The mind is one hell of a thing

Shellon Williams

BookLeaf Publishing

Presentation by *BookLeaf Publishing*

Web: www.bookleafpub.com

E-mail: info@bookleafpub.com

ISBN: 9789357444811

First edition 2023

To those who inspired me and saw the best in me

ACKNOWLEDGEMENT

I would like to acknowledge the extraordinary debt I owe to my family and friends for always pushing me and encouraging me and reminding me that I am destined for greatness even when I felt like I would fail over and over again. Also I would like to thank God for always guiding me through this journey called life, no one said it was going to be easy but we just have to make the best of it . Every trials and rejection I've faced have made me much stronger and much more inspired to be great.

I would like to thank the publishers at book leaf publishing for you made it much easier for me . I would also like to acknowledge and thank anyone that is going to support me in the future.

My little Angel (To my daughter Jamelia)

Before you were out of my womb, I knew you,
Before I saw you I loved you, Those little feet and hands,
That little delicate looking mouth that uttered those silent words, I love you mother,
Which sounds like music to my ears,
Now that you're here, I love you even more,
You are the only precious thing that I've grown to adore, what life meant to me I had no clue,
You are the one who made me want to live on through and through,
Look at you now, as you sleep, With a smile on your face that is mines to keep, I pray that God will guide you and protect you for me,
You are my motivation and you are the key,
Lastnight I had a bad dream and in this dream you weren't there; but when I woke up,
I held you near,
A dream like that I would never want to come through,
If God had to take one of us, that should be me not you, For I have lived my life,
This little angel came from above, and all that's filled in my life is love; pure love

Now it's your turn, No matter what;I will be with you, my angel, to guide you as you learn.

Mindgasm

When he go down, he go down on my mind, undressing my conscience while stimulating my body and soul. If he must suck, He would suck on my thoughts by sliding his tongue into the wetness of my intellect. He gently circle the clit of my emotions, exposing raw feelings of erotic desire, then he tongue my most intimate disclosures.

He soul kiss the entrance of my darkest secrets and gently suck on the nib of my determination. He do this slow and deep, causing an enormous mindgasm that sets my tight place on fire. An experience like no other.

I'm now leaking, my soaking wet panties can no longer hold back the flow of my sweet juice now trickling down my thighs. Hormones raging like a stampede, i'm on the verge of an explosive orgasm. Simply because he kidnapped my thoughts and held my mind hostage with only my intellect

When we collided

When we collided, it couldn't be just a
coincidence or some incident
You came so swiftly and obtained residence in
my space
We fell in love so unexpectedly at a very fast
pace

Who said the race was not for the swift ?
Just thinking about how you cleverly won my
heart over makes me somewhat stiff

Just like a thief within the dawn of night
You broke into my heart with all your might
And now that we've collided, I don't want you
out of my sight
With you, I can clearly see the light

When we first collided, what caught me first
was that never-ending stare
And although other people were looking, you
didn't seem to care
All I know now is that we're the perfect pair
And the truth is I need you as much as I need air

Why I love you

I love you not because of what you do
But for who you are and how you make me feel
I love you so much that these feelings
sometimes feel surreal

I love you because of the silly way you stare
And when I look into your eyes, I know I need
not have any fear

I love you because of how protected you make
me feel
You came into my life at a time when I had little
hope that my heart would ever heal

I love you because of how gentle you are to
every inch of my body
Loving you is my new best hobby

I love you for the simplest things that you do
I don't know where life is gonna take us, but if I
had to do this again, I would always choose you

I love you even when you get me mad
Truth be told, being with you makes me happier
than sad

I love your overall personality
And how you put up with all of my bs
Sorry if I try to make you stress
Just know I mean nothing but the best

I love you because of that amazing humor you have
It gives me such a euphoric feeling that I never had

I love you because you're half man and half amazing
When I feel like my world is caving, the thoughts of you are like my safe Haven

What if I told you ?

As a man, I know that you feel like you can't
express how you feel enough ,
And you probably feel like there isn't any
woman you can even trust
But what if I told you that I can be the woman
you want me to be ?
The one to care and love you unconditionally

What if I told you that i want to be your best
friend ?
Whom you can share your darkest secrets with
that you wouldn't even have to pretend

What if I told you that you could lean on me ?
Let me be your body ;
I know they say that a man is supposed to be the
head
But I believe that without the body, the head is
dead

What if I told you that I don't like it when it
seems as though you're pushing me away?
The truth is it gives me mixed signals that I don't
know whether to leave or stay

What if I told you that I think of you all the
time?
Even the thoughts of our first encounter from
time to time

What if I told you I am worried sick about you?
In ways, I don't even think you have a clue
But I want you to know that I really do love you

What if i told you that I don't believe that a man
should fetch his own weight?
I honestly just think society's beliefs are just so
out of date

What if I told you that I want to share your pain
and hurt
I would never want to be the woman who would
leave you in the dirt
being with me has its perks

What if I told you I want more out of this ?
I hope that after you read this piece, you will get
the gist

Understand ,I am not your average type of
woman, and I would never want to be. I just
want you to love me for me

Soulful Whisper

So now your soul is trying to whisper into mine,
It almost feels like I'm going back in time, The thoughts of our hearts being entwined make me feel like I am losing my mind,

To be or not to be; It's like your soul relates to every inch of me, This euphoric feeling can't be compared to

any type of sexual healing,

It's more like a spiritual ritual that makes

our soul a whole; Making me lose control,

Could this be my soulmate? Am I dreaming? Is this some silly mistake, Haunted by the thoughts that you want me; It's like your soul is out to taunt me,
Truth be told, I want you to touch my body with that your soul.

When I'm with you

When I’m with you sex is more than just the friction between two bodies. It’s an erotic poem beneath the sheets, a sensual encounter way more than just heat and sensation.

When I’m with you sex is all about soul connection, the way my tongue tells you the words I’m not brave enough to utter, how it write my stories of lust on your bare flesh.The way my desire give you the warmth you’ve been yarning for.

When I’m with you sex transcends pleasure. It’s an exploration of our deepest depths together, a dive into unchartered waters. It’s mending our imperfections to create something magical. Something perfect....

The way your passion soaked lips remind me that i'm beautiful from the inside out. That my scars are blooming flowers that you'll continue to kiss and cherish.That no matter what i'm wearing to you i'm always naked and that's what I ever wanted for someone to love me naked not literally but with my flaws and all.

The way you look into my eyes and see
everything I desperately try to hide, and your
kiss will never allow me to forget that i'm an art.
Provocative and raw, deeper than just the surface
and way more than what i'd like to show off.

One sweet day

One sweet day you will realize I love you just
like the flowers that bloom in may
And I hope to be by your side to remind you
every day
That you're amazing in every kind of way

One sweet day, you will come around
I just know that's why I chose to stay
I will wait for you, my love, no matter what
people say

One sweet day.
I hope you let me be your ray of sunlight
When there is too much rain
I promise to brighten your day and take away all
the pain

H.E.R

Damage is what she is, but no one sees that
All they see is her smile and beauty and not the fact
The fact that she -"Her" a mother , daughter, sister, or friend who is constantly fighting daily the demons of the past or present that all she does is pretend
She pretends that she's ok making everyone around her laugh and smile, but behind closed doors, all she does is cry
A cry for help because she feels so much alone
And feels like if she ever tries to speak up, she would be stoned
"Her," that beautiful friend you see not knowing that she is going through hurts and pains
"Her," that daughter that bears all the strain
"Her," that mother that is afraid to face the Shame
"Her" that same beautiful and intelligent woman who you have or had no idea that suicide is one of her aim
She tries so hard to conceal, but the pain is so much that it feels like it would never heal
So she suffers for days or years. Could it be that no one noticed this or no one really cares

Depression that son of a gun that piles up one's
hurts and pain only to mentally take them down .
Sometimes, all it makes them feel is like their
about to drown
I am here to tell you that you are not alone,
queen, so please queen, fix your crown

Woman of Substances

You are a woman of substance
that was beautifully created from dust
Like a delicately put together sculpture
You add value to this earth
You are strong
You are awesome
You are the strength of a man
And the backbone of your family
You are a woman of substance
Even with your flaws, you still manage to
compose yourself
To smile and laugh
You are a superwoman
Even when you're sad, you try your best to make
sure others are okay
You are a woman of worth
A phenomenal woman that's who you are

Just like a glowstick

Just like a glowstick
Just like a glowstick,
he had to break you,
It's not saying that he just wants to hurt you
He broke you because you needed to bend
And see, not everyone is your friend

Just like a glowstick, he broke you so you can glow
Now, looking at your face, your happiness shows
This is just to make you strong enough to endure anything the devil throws

Just like a glowstick
You will start to see changes
But don't you give up this is a part of the cycling stages

Just like a glowstick, you'll soon shine so bright
So don't you ever give anyone that will power to dim your lights

Depression is my name

Hi, my name is Depression
I might come in the form of a family member or a friend
I am so strong that I can decrease any feelings of you thinking that you're enough or was even heaven sent

I am like the devil in disguise. I'll make you question your worth
To a point where I make you feel like dirt
I'll take your hurt and build a home
then rip you apart until you're torn

I came to steal ,kill, and destroy
I'll use you like you're my favorite toy
I'll make you feel like you're alone
You'll feel so lost you'll believe your life was stolen

I'll make you pretend to be happy and make others happy, too
My mission is to gain full control of you
where it's too late for your friends to even have a clue
Just like glue, I 'll be stuck on you

I will go to any extent to make sure
I drain you to a point where you have no more strength
No strength to walk or talk
When I am finish with you , you will be left in the dark

I'll try and try until I succeed
No matter how you beg and plead
I'll try with all my might
To make you lose sight
Until I slowly dim your lights .

A baggage Claim

As I helped him unpack his baggage; I
exposed his darkest secrets ,
The secrets of all the misery he had put her
through I was shaking because I had no clue
Because I was busy playing the role of the other
woman, which was all fun and games
But now, seeing the monster he is, I guess this is
my share
He painted her as a villain
And to contribute to her daily dose of pain, I was
willing
Willing to help him even if it meant that I would
single handedly help to destroy her
Now, I am the newest mockery
It's the same script, but it's a different cast you
see
Because he's been deceiving not only her but me
If only I knew that playing games was his only
aim
Can't believe i've become his baggage claim

Because he sure did drop the weight of his
luggage on me surprisingly

Feels like the universe is now against me

What I didn't know was once I took her place
I made room for my spot to be replaced
Yes, there she was, another woman ready to
accept him while he was also with me
Karma has a funny way of dealing with you ,you
see

I played the role of the side chick
I wish I was a sidekick
To know better that when
He told me I would be his main if I give him
some more time
It was just another one of his manipulating lies
He took all of what's left of my pride
I honestly don't know if I should laugh or cry

She warned me that I would have my day
I laughed at her and told her he loved me more.
There's no way
She told me I am nothing but "a baggage claim "
Sad to say that she was right ;now look at me all
hurt and ashamed
Because I contributed to an innocent woman's
pain
Not everything that glitters is gold
The truth is you shouldn't go meddling in other
people's relationships until the other person's
side is told

Nothing but an anchor

You were nothing more than an anchor to me,
Who was trying to drown me in the deep blue sea
You took and took until I couldn't give anymore
You were like the rough waves on the shore

You are the true epitome of what they called the biggest disaster
Because when it came to causing chaos, you are the master

You took all the laughter
I prefer the before than the after
You left me with only pain and sorrow
I feel like someone shot me with an arrow

You left me in depression mode
You stole my heart and played with it
I can't believe I took that hit
I thought you were Mr. Cool
But once again, I played the fool

The Strong friend

I am a strong friend who is always smiling
I am also the very emotional friend that cries when hiding
I am a supportive friend
The life of the party friend
The ride or die friend
But I am also the silently hurting friend
The friend that feels alone
The friend that fights battles on his/her own
The friend that feels like it's him / her against the world and like the things he/she feels will be judged if it's heard
It's either you're too young,smart or too handsome, or pretty
I really just don't want people's pity
So here I am, concealing how I feel
Just because this world we live in doesn't treat depression like it's real

A Thin line between love and hate

I loved you with all of me, but
Things don't always go as planned, you see;
It was amazing when I first met you ,
Now I am sitting here reminiscing all the things
I've endured, and now I regret you
I am trying my utmost best to forget you

They say there is a thin line between love and
hate
Now I know that meeting you couldn't be my
faith
But I know that true love is out there looking for
me, so I'll wait

The next time I meet the perfect stranger
I'll make sure I guard my heart from danger
Because I put my guards down
For a man who treated me like a circus clown

I am nobody's fool
I really thought you were Mr . Cool
But you are just another chapter of my life of
Meeting Mr. Wrong

It's sad that i still have memories of you when I
hear certain songs

I take it all back ; what I said about hoping to
see a glimpse of us
Cause you showed me that you never really
loved me it was all just lust

I am not going to lie,the honeymoon phase of
when we first met was great
But now my love for you has turned to hate
So now I am putting the love I have for you to
rest
But I wish you and your future endeavors the
very best

Don't let him patronize you

Don't let him patronize you
Stop having him lie to you
Just accept the truth
Nothing that he says is cute
You can't make him love you if he don't
And the truth is you can't make his heart feel something it won't
He is an ass trust me look at all the malnourished treatment your soul suffered in the past
is he really not an a**?
You need to put your vision on contrast
to see clearly the disappointing and unfulfilled promises you experienced in the past.
He just had one task
Just one task
To love and treat you right and make you not only his one and only but his last.
That simple task he could not even pass.
What an a**?

Dear men

Dear men
We are tired of the verbal , emotional, mental and physical abuse
We do not like the feeling of being misused
If we say we want to leave please let us go
We should not have to feel like a prisoner on death row

Birthed by a woman just like me
How can you hurt one and not at all feel guilty?
How sly can you be?
Deceiving your friends
When behind closed doors you're putting that woman through nothing but hell

Some of you men are like the devil in disguise
And it's sad to say some people tend to fall for your covered up manipulating lies
You just expect us women to do or die
Just stop your dry cry

Stop making our women victims of untimely death
Stop doing things to hurt us because in time you'll regret

How can your heart be so cold
Some women's story will forever be untold
Sorry for the loss of these innocent souls
Just because of your feelings you couldn't
control

Men please I beg learn to play your role
We need your protection not to be controlled
We want to be loved and consoled
Not to be apart of the rising murderous death toll

This cruel world just makes it hard to trust
To hurt her means you didn't love her it was all
just lust
I hope you know that you too will one day go
back to dust
Dear men please stop hurting us

What a foolish man?

How could you be so naive or blinded by the fact that her heart is as big as a mansion with many rooms .All you had to do was choose, but no, you refused. All she asked of was for you to listen . You had a place where you can call your home or your comforter. With a kitchen so big that you could've put together the world's best recipe of love .
How dare you refuse the room your soul could have found rest ? How dare you go through that forbidden door ? You had a home that could have made you feel like a king on a throne. What a foolish man? Why did you choose to be homeless?

She got flowers today

She got flowers today
Today of all day when she cooked and she cleaned
He chose to be so mean .
He shouted at her in front of her friends, but when they left, he beat her so bad that the next day, the bruises were so visible that she couldn't even pretend

She got flowers today
Today of all day , he told her he was sorry but then hit her again.
This time, he hitted her even harder.
She kicked, and she screamed yelling baby please ...
All he did was give her one more squeeze
A squeeze to the neck that had her wheezing.
Nothing she did seems to please him

She got flowers today
 only thing this time, she woke up and saw him by her bedside saying sorry again , not her bed but a bed in a cold place called a hospital

The flowers looked like poison ivy because she was in so much misery asking "God please help me."
But she still went back

She got flowers again today, but today was the last day ,the saddest day and the day that wouldn't have happened this way if she didn't agree to stay .
The day she got flowers last was the day she was breathless because he took her life away
So at her funeral she got flowers that day

Butterfly fly Away

You tried to prepare us for this moment
But it's never easy at all
We never knew that shortly we would see
another angel fall

The selfish part of us wanted you to remain a
caterpillar
But we never knew that you would bloom into a
beautiful butterfly

I guess it is true ;what they say when you see a
butterfly flying It's either joy or pain it brings
But I guess God wanted you more, so he had
you gain your wings

Now, when we see a butterfly, we'll think about
the special thoughts
and the battles you fought
For the strength you had couldn't be bought

It hurts so much that you are no longer with us
But even in the trial times in God, we still trust
He knows how much you've endured
He took your pain and exchanged it for wings

Knowing that when we see a butterfly, our heart
will still sing

They say that God's strongest soldier has the
hardest fights
but we saw you throw those punches with all
your might
Go be with those angels, spread your wings, and
shine your light
to us, you will always represent one of the
brightest stars at night

You're at peace now
in no more pain as you sleep
Oh, sweet beloved, please rest in peace

In loving memory of my aunt Rishida Bristol

www.ingramcontent.com/pod-product-compliance
Lightning Source LLC
Chambersburg PA
CBHW051749130826
49812CB00033B/1063
9789357444811